SHOULD THE POSSE COMITATUS ACT BE CHANGED TO EFFECTIVELY SUPPORT LOCAL LAW ENFORCEMENT?

Through much of our nation's history, the Army has played a role in civil law enforcement. At other times, Congress has attempted to limit that role while still providing flexibility to respond to extraordinary circumstances that are beyond a state's capability and require federal assistance. The Posse Comitatus Act is often invoked in discussions about the use of the Armed Forces in civil support operations. Some claim it is an essential constitutional protection from abuse of individuals and the states by federal authorities[1] while others suggest that it is an archaic statute that restricts the President's ability to respond in a crisis and must be amended to support today's circumstances. The truth about Posse Comitatus is somewhere in between: the Posse Comitatus Act was neither intended to protect the citizens from the abuses of the government nor is it inflexible. The original intent was limiting the military's role in the routine exercise of law enforcement operations. This paper will look at what the Posse Comitatus Act actually says, the history of Posse Comitatus, and when it does and does not apply.

Definition

The Posse Comitatus Act was originally passed June 18, 1878 as an amendment to an Army appropriation bill.[2] The National Security Act of 1947, Title 10, Section 375 further directed that the Secretary of Defense publish regulations to ensure that any activity (including providing equipment, facility or personnel) does not include or permit

---

[1] Joe Wolverton II, "Barack Obama Continues Bush Administration Policy Regarding Posse Comitatus," *The New America Magazine*, October 30, 2009,Available from: http://www.thenewamerican.com/index.php/usnews/politics/2195-barack-obama-continues-bush-administration-policy-regarding-posse-comitatus, Accessed: February 15, 2011.
[2] Charles Doyle, The Posse Comitatus Act & Related Matters: The Use of the Military to Execute Civilian Law, *Congressional Research Service*, Washington DC: The Library of Congress, 2000, p 43,

direct participation by a member of the Army and Air Force in a search, seizure, arrest, or other similar activity unless authorized by law.[3] It was not until 1956 that Congress amended the Posse Comitatus Act to include the Air Force and moved the Act to Title 18, United States Code (USC), Section 1385, stating: "Whoever, except in cases and under circumstances expressly authorized by the Constitution or an act of Congress, willfully uses any part of the Army or Air Force as a Posse Comitatus or otherwise to execute the laws shall be fined under this title or imprisoned not more than two years, or both."[4] Although the Posse Comitatus Act does not address the Navy or Marine Corps, by Department of Defense directives and regulations they are under the same restrictions as the Army and Air Force.

United States Northern Command (NORTHCOM), whose mission encompasses Homeland Defense and Civil Support operations like defending, protecting, and securing the United States, interprets this to mean that U.S. military personnel are prohibited from direct participation in routine law enforcement activities. These activities include interdicting vehicles, vessels, and aircraft; conducting surveillance, searches, pursuit and seizures; or making arrests on behalf of civilian law enforcement authorities (NORTHCOM, Mission).[5]NORTHCOM goes on to state, "prohibiting direct military involvement in law enforcement is in keeping with long-standing U.S. law and policy limiting the military's role in domestic affairs."[6]

It is generally accepted that Posse Comitatus does not apply to the Army and Air Force National Guard while serving under state control because they operate under Title

---

[3]10 United States Code (U.S.C.) §375
4 10 U.S.C. §1385
[5]United States Northern Command, Missions, Available from:
http://www.northcom.mil/About/history_education/vision html, Accessed: March 2, 2011.
[6]Ibid.

32 authority and not Title 10 authority.[7] Since the Posse Comitatus Act does not apply to National Guard units while under state control, state governors have the flexibility to use guardsmen for law enforcement and in support of law enforcement missions. Once federalized, however, National Guard forces are subject to Title 10 and the Posse Comitatus Act.[8] As a result states are reluctant to allow their forces to be called to active federal service during disasters like Hurricane Katrina.[9]

History

Posse Comitatus is Latin for "power of the country" or the "force of the country."[10] Its roots lie in English law of 1411 that allowed the Sheriff to utilize all citizens above the age of 15 to maintain order. It was considered a duty as a citizen, eventually evolving into the creation of local militias as England colonized North America.[11]

The 1770 Boston Massacre by British soldiers, the practice of quartering British troops in colonial homes without the owner's permission prior to and during the American Revolutionary, and the threatened overthrow of the new American government by the American Army in 1783 all led to mistrust of large standing armies. This resulted in constitutional limitations on the Army.[12] These limitations included the constitutionally directed civilian Commander-in-Chief[13] and Congress being "solely

---

[7] Jennifer Elsea, The Posse Comitatus Act and Related Matters: A Sketch, *Congressional Research Service*, (Washington DC, The Library of Congress, 2005), p. 4.
[8] Ibid, p. 5.
[9] Bush, George W., *Decision Points*, (New York, Crown, November 9, 2010), p. 320.
[10] *The Oxford American Dictionary*, 3rd ed., (New York, Oxford University Press, 2010), p. 1365.
[11] Ibid, p. 1365.
[12] Richard H. Kohn, "The Inside History of the Newburgh Conspiracy: America and the Coup d'état", *The William and Mary Quarterly* (April 1970): 187-220.
[13] U.S. Constitution, Art.II, §2.

empowered to raise and support Armies."[14] The Third Amendment of the Bill of Rights

limits the quartering of troops in private homes.[15] The mistrust of large standing armies

was also one of the reasons often cited for the Second Amendment which states "a well

regulated militia, being necessary to the security of a free state, the right of the people to

keep and bear arms, shall not be infringed."[16]

While limiting the Army, Congress also saw the need for the Army to support law

enforcement and domestic operations. In August 1786, a private militia was formed to

prevent the courts from collecting legal debt and seizing property from debtors.[17] Though

ultimately defeated by militia loyal to the state government, Shays' Rebellion was the

impetus to replace the articles of confederation.[18]With Shays' Rebellion fresh in their

minds, the Constitution writers granted authority for Congress "to provide for calling

forth the militia to execute the laws of the union, suppress insurrections and repel

invasions."[19]

Soon after the1787 ratification of the United States Constitution soon led to

another challenge to federal authority was exercised with the passage of the Excise Tax

Act in 1791.[20] The authority of the federal government was challenged in the Whiskey

Rebellion (also called the Whiskey Insurrection) in areas of western Pennsylvania. While

President Washington was initially cautious in his response, he was forced to react after

---

[14]U.S. Constitution, Art. I, §8.
[15] U.S. Constitution, Am III.
[16] U.S. Constitution, Am II.
17*Encyclopedia of World Biography*, 2004 ed., Daniel Shay, Available from
http://www.encyclopedia.com/doc/1G2-3404705912.html, Accessed March 26, 2011
[18] Ibid.
[19] U.S. Constitution, Art I, §8.
[20]*Encyclopedia of World Biography*, 2004 ed., Whiskey Rebellion, Available from
http://www.encyclopedia.com/topic/Whiskey_Rebellion.aspx, Accessed March 26, 2011.

an attack on a federal tax collector, a rising national debt, and respect for federal authority waning.[21]

The Supreme Court ruled that the laws of the United States were opposed by forces too powerful for the Marshal of the District to enforce. Although suppressing the rebellion in 1794 did not require physical force, the mobilization of more than 10,000 militia from several states shows the federal government's early willingness to use the Army to support laws when the opposition was too powerful for local law enforcement. [22] The federal government's use of the Army in the Whiskey Rebellion, however, was not the first option and came with restrictions. Only after issuing a proclamation and sending commissions to the troubled areas was the Army sent to enforce the laws. Even then it was instructed to issue another proclamation inviting good citizens and friends of the law to join the United States.[23] Following the Whiskey Rebellion subsequent presidents have utilized military forces to suppress riots, which will be discussed in more detail later.

Posse Comitatus again came into play prior to the Civil War when the Army was used to enforce the Fugitive Slave Act of 1850. Since local law enforcement in the northern free states were reluctant, or refused, to enforce the Fugitive Slave Act, the Army was used as a Posse Comitatus to capture and return fugitive slaves.[24] In 1854, Attorney General Cushing published what became known as the Cushing Doctrine, stating that the Posse Comitatus included everyone older then fifteen years whether

[21] Ibid.
[22] Matt Matthews, "The Posse Comitatus Act and the United States Army: A Historic Perspective", *Global War on Terrorism Occasional Paper 14*, (Combat Studies Institute Press, 2006), p. 10.
[23] Ibid, p. 11.
[24] Charles Doyle, The Posse Comitatus Act & Related Matters: The Use of the Military to Execute Civilian Law, *Congressional Research Service*, Washington DC: The Library of Congress, 2000, p. 7.

civilians, military, militia, soldiers, or marines with all required to obey the sheriff or marshal.[25]

Following the Civil War, the U.S. Army was utilized to help enforce civil rights in the former Confederate states. Organized violence and oppression were used to limit the ability of blacks to vote and govern. The Army was sent to the southern states to secure polling positions and protect citizens from the Ku Klux Klan. With the polling stations secure, the blacks and Republicans were able to win southern election. [26]

Needless to say, using the Army for law enforcement in the former Confederate states was not popular. Therefore, following the contested election of President Rutherford B. Hayes in 1876, a large portion of the Army was ordered out of the South.[27] With the Army removed from overseeing polling stations and restraining the oppression of blacks and Republicans, one state after another quickly fell to the white Democrats. Once in power southern Democrats worked to end any participation by blacks in southern politics.[28]

The original Posse Comitatus Act, Army Appropriation bill, Chapter 263, Section 15, originated under these circumstances and was approved in 1878. Passage was carried in large part by southern Democrats who controlled the House of Representatives. The Senate, controlled by Republicans, also passed it. While some contend correctly, that Posse Comitatus was the South's attempt to gain revenge on the Army for its occupation of the South during and after the Civil War, the federal government was also wary of

---

[25]Gary Felicetti and John Luce, "The Posse Comitatus Act: Liberation from the Lawyers", *Parameters* (Autumn 2004): p. 94-107.
[26]Matt Matthews, "The Posse Comitatus Act and the United States Army: A Historic Perspective", *Global War on Terrorism Occasional Paper 14*, (Combat Studies Institute Press, 2006), p. 31.
[27]Ibid, p. 31.
[28]Ibid, p. 32.

U.S. Marshals and local sheriffs pressing the Army into service without the Commander-in-Chief's approval. While there may be debate about the motivations for passage of the Posse Comitatus Act, it is in many ways irrelevant since it remains the law of the land.

When the Posse Comitatus Act Does and Does Not Apply

Violation of Posse Comitatus cannot occur when the Constitution expressly authorizes the use of the Army or Air Force as a Posse Comitatus to execute the law, when Congress or the President expressly authorizes use of the Army or Air Force as a Posse Comitatus, or when the activity does not involve execution of the law. Stated another way, violations of Posse Comitatus occur when the Armed Forces perform tasks that are not normally assigned to them and are the role of civilian government, usually state and local law enforcement.[29]

Over the years, Congress has also granted a number of exceptions to Posse Comitatus allowing a limited role for law enforcement. Title 10 USC, Sections 331-335, the Insurrection Act, allows the President to authorize the U.S. military to suppress insurrections. It also allows for the use of Soldiers on federal status to enforce federal laws for rebellions against U.S. authorities.[30] Title 10 USC, Sections 371-381, allows for counter drug operations and assistance.[31] Title 18 USC, Section 831 and Section 382, states that when an emergency situation exists in relation to weapons of mass destruction (WMD), the military can assist the Justice Department in enforcing prohibitions regarding WMD materials.[32] In recent years, the Posse Comitatus Act has had an impact on the Armed Force's support to law enforcement including the Los Angeles riots; The

---

[29] Jennifer Elsea, The Posse Comitatus Act and Related Matters: A Sketch, *Congressional Research Service*, Washington DC: The Library of Congress, 2005, p. 3.
[30] Ibid, p. 3.
[31] 10 U.S.C. §371-381
[32] 18 U.S.C. §831 and 382

World Trade Organization Conference in Seattle; and recently, a case involving Military Police assisting local law enforcement in Alabama.

LA Riots

During the afternoon of April 29th, 1992 in Los Angeles (LA) California, an all-white jury acquitted four white police officers of beating Rodney King, a black man who had been apprehended after a high-speed pursuit. Local media outlets repeatedly broadcast King's video taped beating, at the hands of LA police officers that afternoon. That combined with news of the acquittal served as a catalyst for the riots that followed.[33] When outnumbered police officers retreated from rioters in front of a national television audience it further exacerbated the situation and within hours there was massive looting and mayhem throughout south central Los Angeles.

By that evening, at the request of the LA Mayor Tom Bradley, Governor Pete Wilson ordered the mobilization of 2,000 soldiers from the California Army National Guard (CAARNG).[34] By 3:00 the next morning, April30th, the guardsmen had assembled in their armories. But, there were also already 10 dead and over 600 fires in LA by this time.[35] That afternoon at a meeting of senior California law enforcement officials, it was decided that the California Highway Patrol would be used to protect firefighters who were being attacked by rioters. LA Police Chief Daryl Gates asked the CAARNG to

[33]William W. Mendel. *Combat in Cities: The LA Riots and Operation Rio.* , Fort Leavenworth, KS: Foreign Military Studies Office, July 1996. Available from: http://fmso.leavenworth.army mil/documents/rio.htm, Accessed: June 6, 2011.

[34] Matt Matthews, "The Posse Comitatus Act and the United States Army: A Historic Perspective", *Global War on Terrorism Occasional Paper 14*, (Combat Studies Institute Press, 2006), p. 47.

[35] Major General James D. Delk, *Fires and Furies: The L.A. Riots, What Really Happened*, (Etc Publications, 1994), p. 64

"handle everything else."[36] The first CAARNG units arrived on the streets shortly thereafter.

Due to the chaos and large area of operations it was difficult to centrally command and control the CAARNG units. In response, National Guard unit commanders at all levels sought out local police stations and performed whatever missions they were asked to perform. To simplify command and control the CAARNG aligned military unit boundaries with police jurisdictional boundaries.[37] While this system was ad hoc, it was effective in supporting local law enforcement requirements. The situation improved with the arrival of thousands of guardsmen, however, due to poor situational awareness and lack of clear communications, Governor Pete Wilson requested federal troops on May1st.[38] That same day, the President ordered 4,000 active duty Soldiers and Marines to LA under the authority of the Insurrection Act.[39]

On 1, May President George H.W. Bush issued a Proclamation followed by an Executive Order that stated that the Armed Forces would be used to suppress violence and to restore law and order.[40] Under the Insurrection Act, the restrictions on the active duty military under the Posse Comitatus Act do not apply. This may not have been clear, however, to the newly appointed Joint Task Force-Los Angeles (JTF-LA) commander Major General (MG) Marvin L. Covault, who also commanded the 7th Infantry Division

[36]Major General James D. Delk, *The 1992 Los Angeles Riots: Military Operations in Los Angeles*, Available from: http://www.militarymuseum.org/HistoryKingMilOps.html. Accessed: February 17, 2011.

[37] Christopher M. Schnaubel, "Lessons in Command and Control from the Los Angeles Riots", *Parameters* (Summer 1997), p. 88-109

[38] Matthews, p. 49

[39]Mendel.

[40] President George W. Bush, *Executive Order 12804,Providing for the Restoration of Law and Order in the City and County of Los Angeles, and Other Districts of California*, Available from: http://www.presidency.ucsb.edu/ws/index.php?pid=23739#axzz1LJ8asCHJ, Accessed: May 3, 2011.

(Light) at Fort Ord, California.[41] Under the Insurrection Act, the President ordered the CAARNG federalized and placed under the command of JTF-LA and no longer under the command of the state governor. Police Chief Gates and LA County Sheriff Block had planned to utilize the active duty soldiers in the same manner as they had successfully used the CAARNG, in direct support of law enforcement.

At their first meeting, MG Couvault informed the surprised Chief and Sheriff that Active Duty units and the now federalized CAARNG units would no longer support or perform civil law enforcement duties.[42] Matt Matthews in his Combat Studies Institute Occasional Paper makes the case that MG Couvault and his staff did not understand what the President's proclamation said and had a weak understanding of the Posse Comitatus Act.[43] A former Staff Judge Advocate for the United States Special Operations Command and noted expert on the Posse Comitatus Act, Colonel (Retired) Thomas R. Lujan, states, "The JTF commander may have had political, policy, or tactical reasons for refusing law enforcement missions, but his asserted reliance on the proscription of Posse Comitatus was misplaced."[44] The JTF-LA headquarters also appears to have been risk adverse. Once JTF-LA was in charge of all military forces responding to the LA riots, they issued arming orders that required all weapons to be carried sling arms with ammo stowed.[45] This after the CAARNG had already shown good fire discipline for four days while on the streets through the worst of the riots with only 20 rounds expended.[46]

[41] Matthews, p. 52-54.
[42] Ibid, p. 54.
[43] Ibid, p. 54.
[44] Ibid, p. 57.
[45] Mendel.
[46] Delk, http://www.militarymuseum.org/HistoryKingMilOps.html.

Regardless of the reason for the JTF-LA commander's refusal to perform law enforcement missions, the result was that requests for military support of law enforcement dropped from nearly 100% approval to only 20 percent.[47] Major General Delk states that after a joint meeting was held by state law enforcement officers, they concluded that the request for of federal troops was a mistake that severely limited their flexibility and the type of missions they were able to undertake.[48] JTF-LA further complicated command and control by redrawing unit boundaries that were not aligned with police jurisdictions.[49] While no one has asserted that federalization prolonged the riots, the perceived restriction on federal military forces due to a limited understanding of the Posse Comitatus Act did restrict use of military forces where no restrictions existed previously under state control.

Seattle 1999 — <u>World Trade Organization</u>

The World Trade Organization (WTO) Ministerial Conference was held in Seattle between November 29th and December 3rd, 1999. The WTO is an international agency with 134 member nations that assists in overseeing international trade rules. Its purpose is to assist in the flow of trade through a system based on rules and to settle disputes. Despite heavy security, the previous WTO Ministerial Conference in Geneva, Switzerland in May 1998 encountered large protests, looting, property damages, and clashes with police.[50] By as early as June 1999, the FBI issued a threat assessment stating that there was a "strong indication" of considerable protest activity for the Seattle

---

[47]Delk, p. 307.
[48]Ibid, p. 396.
[49]Schnaubel, p. 88-109.
[50] The Seattle Police Department, *The Seattle Police Department, After Action Report, World Trade Ministerial Conference Seattle Washington, November 29 – December 3, 1999*, April 4, 2000, p. 9-10.

conference.[51] As the conference date approached, additional reports indicated plans for arson and takeover of corporate offices. Despite these indicators Seattle Mayor Paul Schell, wanted to allow the demonstrators to be able to liberally exercise their right to protest based on Seattle's history of peaceful protest and respect for others property. With this view as planning guidance and resource concerns (costs) the Seattle Police Department (SPD) failed to plan for a worst-case scenario occurring during the conference.[52]

The first protest occurred on Saturday, November 27th, 1999 and was peaceful and very limited in size. Sunday, November 30th saw protest that numbered in the hundreds and minor property damage. On Monday, November29th, there were several marches as large as 1,000 and more vandalism. When a group threatened to take over Niketown retail store they were told by other protestors to "keep it peaceful today. Today is not the day to break windows. Wait until tomorrow."[53] By the morning of November30th, the protestors showed their true intentions and organization.

Well-coordinated groups converged from multiple directions on the downtown core area and began erecting barriers, starting fires and blocking 14 intersections. By 0800, protestors breached one of the conference venues and assaulted WTO delegates. At another venue, the police commander reported that he was loosing control of the situation. Protestors were also donning gas masks and spraying police with chemical irritants.[54] While these acts were occurring, police were still required to man their posts at the various venues and escort numerous protests previously approved and issued permits

---

[51]Ibid, p. 18.
[52]Ibid, p. 5.
[53]Ibid, p. 36.
[54]Ibid, p. 39.

by the city which numbered as large as 40,000, organized by the AFL-CIO, all of which severely stressed police resources. At3:32 pm Mayor Schell declared a Civil Emergency and an Emergency Order imposing a curfew.[55]

By approximately 4:00 pm, the state Joint Operation Center (JOC) at Washington Army National Guard (WAARNG) headquarters (HQ) at Camp Murray near Tacoma was telephonically notified that the Governor had authorized the activation of the WAARNG. Over the next several minutes they were told that they might be needed, they would require one battalion on standby, they would need two battalions on stand by, and, finally, that they required two battalions immediately.[56]For civil support mission purposes, each battalion was called a Response Task Force (RTF) and was augmented with various resources that were tailored for civil support missions. In addition to these two RTFs, an Infantry Brigade HQ and State JOC were activated for command and control and liaison functions. Soldiers were assembled in their armories, one each north and south of Seattle, and moved to the Seattle Armory during the night of November30th. By first light on December1st, soldiers were on the streets of Seattle.[57]

Solders from the two RTFs were organized into four man teams with each team being pared with a police officer. The committed RTFs were placed under the operational control (OPCON) of the Seattle Police while three other RTFs were placed on alert but not assembled and held under state control.

The SPD primarily used the RTF soldiers to man checkpoints and as a show of force throughout the downtown core. The Posse Comitatus Act did not apply to the WAARNG Soldiers during this period since they were on state active duty orders. Under

[55]Ibid, p. 41.
[56]LTC (Retired) Timothy J. Woodard, 81steSIB S-2, telephone interview with author March 11, 2011.
[57] Ibid.

state active duty status the state pays for the soldiers and exercises command and control over them. This is distinct from even their normal drill status, Title 32, where the federal government covers the costs but they are under state control. Although the Posse Comitatus Act was not applicable to these soldiers, the SPD decided that all arrests would be made by law enforcement personnel and not by military personnel.

The soldiers were available to assist the police officers. But, the restriction was put in place because of the level of training required to make arrests that could be successfully prosecuted in court. It was not due to any federal or state restrictions.[58] The WAARNG RTFs were successfully employed in this manner until early morning of December2nd.

At this point, the SPD shifted tactics in regards to the use of the WAARNG and employed them in platoon riot formations as barriers to the protestors. Their first use was to relieve the SPD's East Precinct which was then under siege by protestors. Until this point, rioters were unwilling to physically engage the soldiers under any circumstance. The East Precinct would be the first time the riots decided to challenge them.[59]

It was a swift and hard lesson for the rioters. The protestors charged the WAARNG line and were met with riot batons. From then on the rioters were content to heckle the soldiers from a distance and the siege of the precinct ended without further incidents. The rest of December 2nd saw a de-escalation of demonstrations and with the SPD now having personnel from surrounding departments and the RTFs, they were sufficiently resourced to respond to any incident. At 6:00 a.m. on December 4, the RTFs

---

[58] Ibid.
[59] Ibid.

and assisting law enforcement agencies were relieved of their duty and began to return to their home stations.[60]

Since the WAARNG was under state authority during the entire WTO incident, the Posse Comitatus Act never was a factor. The RTFs were able to assemble quickly, once called, and employed without delay. While lawyers are a part of any strategic decision today, there was no confusion with respect to how or if the soldiers could be employed. Political considerations in the decision to employ forces were simplified since all the officials involved were local and state officials. Finally, the WAARNG soldiers enjoyed considerable popularity with the general public throughout the employment since they were "our boys" and were there to assist those in need. Never were they seen as an outside force. One indicator of the popularity of the Soldiers was the large number of phone numbers the male Soldiers received from single females that worked in the downtown core.[61]

Samson, Alabama — March 2009

On March 10 2009 in Samson Alabama, twenty-two Fort Rucker Military Police (MP) assisted the Samson police department for five hours after Michael McLendon killed 10 people in a murder spree.[62] The MPs responded after the local Sheriff asked for assistance, due to the small size of his department and the immense effort it would take them to collect evidence at the numerous crime scenes.[63] The MP manned traffic control points, secured crime scenes and never made any arrests. A Department of the Army

---

[60] Seattle Police Department, p. 47.

[61] Woodard.

[62] Associated Press, *Troop use After Ala. Shootings Illegal,* October 20, 2009, Available fromhttp://www.military.com/news/article/troop-use-after-ala-shootings-illegal.html on February 12, 2011.Accessed June 6, 2011.

[63] Gina Cavallaro, Soldiers help reviewed after Ala. Shooting, *Army Times*, March 28, 2009, Available from: http://www.armytimes.com/news/2009/03/army_rucker_032809w/, Accessed: March 3, 2011.

Inspector General report released to the Associated Press in October 2009 concluded that despite the good intentions of the Army unit, the deployment of troops was a violation of the Posse Comitatus Act.[64] The person who approved the deployment of soldiers to assist the Samson Police Department claimed he did so based on his previous experience with military assisting civilians during hurricanes Katrina and Andrew. He was administrative punished for his mistake.[65]

Without a request by the state governor and approval by the President, federal forces cannot assist in law enforcement activities. Exceptions are provided for training civilian law enforcement and use of equipment. Lack of knowledge of the law has never worked as a defense for criminals in the courtroom and in this case it did not for a well-intentioned but poorly educated soldier in command of the Fort Rucker's MPs. Although this was a minor incident compared to LA or WTO riots, it highlights the lack of understanding and education of the Posse Comitatus Act by elements of the active duty Armed Forces.

Command and Control Issues

A common criticism of the Posse Comitatus Act is that it creates difficulties with command and control when federal forces are employed. In the 2006 lessons learned report on the federal response to Hurricane Katrina, Frances Townsend points out that there were several separate chains of command operating simultaneously.[66] This resulted in duplication of effort and wasted resources and time. The report points out that even the federal government could not coordinate its own resources since there is not statutory

---

[64]Associated Press.
[65]Ibid.
[66]Frances F. Townsend, *The Federal Response to Hurricane Katrina: Lessons Learned, Recommendation 55*, February 23, 2006, Available from: http://georgewbush-whitehouse.archives.gov/reports/katrina-lessons-learned, Accessed February 17, 2011.

authority within the federal government to place all resources under a single chain of command.[67] This lack of coordination at the federal level has nothing to do with the Posse Comitatus Act. Ms. Townsend developed 122 recommendations in her report and discusses extensively the lack of coordination, lack of a common operating picture and separate reporting channels.[68] Despite her comprehensive recommendations, Townsend does not recommend any changes to the Posse Comitatus Act. The report concludes that the lack of a single command structure inhibited the unity of effort between the federal forces and the state National Guard formation.

Many papers recommend that the Posse Comitatus Act must be revised to allow for the active duty military to have command and control over National Guard formations. This is not an acceptable solution to many states and local governments due to political and state sovereignty principles.[69] In the aftermath of Hurricane Katrina then President George W. Bush repeatedly tried to persuade Louisiana Governor Kathleen Blanco to request federal forces to assist. She consistently resisted giving up state authority.[70] At the same time the governor had asked for and was receiving thousands of National Guard soldiers from around the country, she had no opposition to assistance, she was just resistant to federal military forces in command of the response in her state.

Governor Blanco even rejected a proposal to allow a unified command to report to both the Governor and the federal government[71]. Even if the Federal government did not have any restriction from the Posse Comitatus Act, it would still not have a single chain of command. Local first responders report to their separate local government

---

[67] Townsend, p. 52.
[68] Townsend, p. 29.
[69] Bush, p. 320.
[70] Bush, p. 323.
[71] Ibid, p. 323.

entities and jurisdictions. There is no authority to place them under military or federal authority. The lack of a single chain of command does not necessarily hamper unity of effort.

At a panel discussion at CSIS on 16 November 2010, Coast Guard Admiral (Retired) Thad Allen[72]did not support Townsend's position. He claims that while there wasn't a single chain of command, there was a unity of effort. He stated that all four of the major players, state and local government, the Coast Guard, the federal government agencies and DOD, all met regularly and coordinated their actions.[73]

Local first responders operate under an incident command system and have mutual aid/assistance agreements in place to ensure they are able to respond to varying levels of incidents. While this is a foreign concept to the military, it is a system that works and meets local first responder's requirements. In the three cases cited above, LA, WTO and Samson, there was unity of effort with local law enforcement. The only time there was a breakdown was when the CAARNG was federalized during the LA riots.

The ARNG has proposed a solution to chain of command issues. In the rare events that require federal forces, the National Guard proposes allowing federal forces to be placed under the authority of the state National Guard leadership.[74] This would simplify chain of command issues and insure unity of effort. While this may seem a radical solution to some, it has been successfully employed in the past. In 2004 this arrangement was used for the G-8 Summit, The Democratic National Convention, The

---

[72] Admiral (Retired) Thad W. Allen, Center for Strategic and International Studies Panel Discussion, Washington DC, November 16, 2010.
[73] Allen.
[74]Lowenburg, Timothy J., MG, The Adjutant General for Washington State National Guard, *The Role of the National Guard in National Defense and Homeland Security*, Available from: http://www.ngaus.org/ngaus/files/ccLibraryFiles/Filename/000000000457/primer%20fin.pdf, Accessed April 9, 2011.

Republican National Convention, and Operation Winter Freeze (supporting the US

Border patrol along the U.S-Canada border).[75] Every state now has a Joint Forces

Headquarters with liaison officers from the active duty military already in place.

In his paper titled *The Role of the National Guard in National Defense and Homeland Security*, Major General Lowenburg states Governors should have command and control of all military forces engaged in emergency and security operations within their state.[76]Duel status authority, Title 10 and Title 32, require the authorization of the President and the state Governor.[77] Most state Adjutant General's (TAGs) are federally recognized general officers that routinely operate under state authority (Title 32) and federal (Title 10) orders. Reversing the roles is not as simple since active duty general officers are not recognized by the states as having state commissions and, therefore, cannot command Title 32 forces or forces on state active duty.

In her report, Townsend supports this position and states:

> The JTF should assume command and control of federal active duty forces and National Guard forces from other states. As part of the JFHQ State, the JTF maintains and provides trained and equipped forces and capabilities. If and when necessary, this JTF model enables a National Guard commander familiar with state and local area of operations to serve both in a federal and state status providing both unity of effort and unity of command for Federal and State forces.[78]

Conclusions

Many argue that the Posse Comitatus Act is flawed since it restricts the federal

government in times of crisis. These critics fail to understand that the Posse Comitatus

---

[75]Lowenburg, p. 6.
[76]Ibid, p. 6.
[77]Ibid, p. 6.
[78]Frances F. Townsend, *The Federal Response to Hurricane Katrina: Lessons Learned, Recommendation 29*, February 23, 2006, Available from: http://georgewbush-whitehouse.archives.gov/reports/katrina-lessons-learned, Accessed February 17, 2011.

Act's purpose was to restrict the federal government in all but extraordinary circumstances. This does not mean that it is inflexible or that congress has not adapted the Act to modern situation.

The Posse Comitatus Act allows each state to determine when and if it requires resources beyond its capabilities, as designed. Earlier in the nation's history, when the local government's resources were limited, the active duty military was required to augment limited state resources. Today, states possess a vast array of law enforcement capabilities that are augmented by mutual assistance agreements with other departments.

All states and territories also possess National Guard formations. In circumstances where the state exceeds its available National Guard capacity, it can be augmented with other state National Guard units, without restrictions imposed by the Posse Comitatus Act. Given these capabilities, it is increasing unlikely that states will require federal law enforcement augmentations. The principle of state sovereignty[79] is still an issue in many states and whether one agrees with this concept or not, it is a reality in the decision-making of state authorities. When active duty forces responded to law enforcement needs in the LA riots, the federal government's response hampered law enforcement.

With the states' significant capability to respond to emergencies with National Guard forces, they do not have to be concerned about restrictions that are placed on federal forces. It is only after the states resources are exhausted that the federal government is needed to assist the states as a last resort. The Posse Comitatus Act does allow for the federal government to respond, if requested and the ability to augment law enforcement if the circumstances justify it.

---

[79] Bush, p. 320

Active duty forces train for the full spectrum of war. While some of these missions may seem similar to civilian law enforcement that does not mean that they are. It is important for active duty forces to have the proper training and education prior to being employed in domestic law enforcement support. If federal forces are not trained then it is understandable that they will be reluctant to engage in that mission. This could result in situations like the LA riots where they hamper rather than help local law enforcement efforts.

For non-law enforcement missions, the Department of Defense has repeatedly proven that it is capable of effectively responding to national emergencies within the law. When its vast resources are required and the Department of Defense is given the mission to respond by the President (as in the case of Hurricane Katrina), it can do so quickly and effectively. When asked to support law enforcement missions, active duty forces must recognize that it may need to adapt to the local situation and not expect the locals to adapt to it. The incident command system is in place and will not change. The states feel they understand their land and people better than anyone else and want to be in charge of any response. Local politics drive decisions that the active component must work within if they are to be effective. Finally, it is possible to have unity of effort without a formal chain of command.

Despite its long history the Posse Comitatus Act is still often misunderstood. Whether it is the unnecessary restriction placed on soldiers during the LA riots or the employment of soldiers in a law enforcement capacity in Samson, Alabama, it is clear that the active Army does not fully understand what the Posse Comitatus Act says and intends. The array of amendments and exceptions does not simplify understanding.

Its intent in limiting the military's role in domestic affairs, however, is still sound. The country has changed significantly since the Posse Comitatus Act was first passed but capabilities at the local and state level have also increased significantly since then. The Posse Comitatus Act still affords the President and Congress the flexibility to respond to extraordinary events. Whether Congress determines that it needs to retain, adapt or jettison the Pose Comitatus Act remains to be seen. In the meantime, military commanders at all levels have an obligation to understand the Posse Comitatus Act.

Recommendations

Given the lack of clarity surrounding the Posse Comitatus Act, I recommend that national leaders and the United States Army consider the following:

1) Military commanders and Judge Advocate General lawyers must be trained in the Posse Comitatus Act. We will rarely know when or if the active component will be employed in support to civilian law enforcement. Therefore, a basic understanding of the Posse Comitatus Act is necessary ahead of time. This training must include the statute, history, policies, and regulations that govern the Posse Comitatus Act. Commanders should also have a basic understanding of what the incident response system is and recognize that they must work within that system since they will not ever have command and control of its assets.

Commanders also need to realize that the National Guard units in each state understand how to support local governments better the active duty units. Most state Guard units have extensive experience in responding to floods, fires, large public gatherings, etc. Further, they have plans on how to respond to an array of domestic incidents since this is one of their core missions. This knowledge and experience should be taken advantage of and not restricted.

2) Allow active duty units to serve under state control. This will make it easier for local governments to ask for federal help when they need it. The state National Guard commanders know the geography and the people. They know who the decision makers are in local governments and have the relationships to make the right things happen. For this to work properly it cannot happen ad hoc. Authorities, agreements and planning should be completed ahead of time so there is no time lost when the need arises.

3) Leave the Posse Comitatus Act in place. The Posse Comitatus Act has served this nation well for nearly a century and a half. It embodies the principles of the Constitution, state sovereignty, due process, limited federal intervention, and mistrust of a large standing army. It allows the president to respond when requested and to do so quickly and effectively.

Bibliography

Allen, Thad W., Admiral (Retired), Center for Strategic and International Studies Panel Discussion, Washington DC, November 16, 2010.

Associated Press, *Troop use After Ala. Shootings Illegal,* October 20, 2009, Available fromhttp://www.military.com/news/article/troop-use-after-ala-shootings-illegal.html on February 12, 2011. Accessed June 6, 2011

Bush, George W., President, *Decision Points*, New York, Crown, November 9, 2010.

Bush, George W., President, *Executive Order 12804, Providing for the Restoration of Law and Order in the City and County of Los Angeles, and Other Districts of California*, Available from: http://www.presidency.ucsb.edu/ws/index.php?pid=23739#axzz1LJ8asCHJ, Accessed: May 3, 2011.

Cavallaro, Gina., Soldiers help reviewed after Ala. Shooting, *Army Times*, March 28, 2009, Available from: http://www.armytimes.com/news/2009/03/army_rucker_032809w/Accessed: March 3, 2011.

Delk, James D., Major General (Retired), *Fires and Furies: The L.A. Riots, What Really Happened*, Etc Publications, 1994.

Delk, James D Major General (Retired), *The 1992 Los Angeles Riots: Military Operations in Los Angeles*, Available from: http://www.militarymuseum.org/HistoryKingMilOps.html. Accessed: February 17, 2011.

Doyle, Charles. The Posse Comitatus Act & Related Matters: The Use of the Military to Execute Civilian Law, *Congressional Research Service*, Washington DC: The Library of Congress, 2000.

Elsea, Jennifer K., The Posse Comitatus Act and Related Matters: A Sketch, *Congressional Research Service*, Washington DC: The Library of Congress, 2005.

Encyclopedia of World Biography, 2004, Daniel Shay. Available from: http://www.encyclopedia.com/doc/1G2-3404705912.html, Accessed: June 6, 2011.

Encyclopedia of World Biography, 2004, Whiskey Rebellion, Available from: http://www.encyclopedia.com/topic/Whiskey_Rebellion.aspx, Accessed: March 26, 2011.

Felicetti, Gary and John Luce, "The Posse Comitatus Act: Liberation from the Lawyers", *Parameters,* Autumn 2004: 94-107.

Kohn, Richard H. "The Inside History of the Newburgh Conspiracy: America and the Coup d'état", *The William and Mary Quarterly,* April 1970: 187-220.

Lowenburg, Timothy J., Major General, The Adjutant General for Washington State National Guard, National Guard Association of the United States, *The Role of the National Guard in National Defense and Homeland Security.* Available from: http://www.ngaus.org/ngaus/files/ccLibraryFiles/Filename/000000000457/primer%20fin.pdf.Accessed: February 20, 2011.

Matthews, Matt. "The Posse Comitatus Act and the United States Army: A Historic Perspective", *Global War on Terrorism Occasional Paper 14*, Combat Studies Institute Press, 2006.

Mendel, William W., *Combat in Cities: The LA Riots and Operation Rio.* , Fort Leavenworth, KS: Foreign Military Studies Office, July 1996. Available from: http://fmso.leavenworth.army.mil/documents/rio.htm, Accessed: June 6, 2011.

The Oxford Companion to Law. Oxford: Clarendon Press, 1980.

The Seattle Police Department, After Action Report, World Trade Ministerial Conference: Seattle Washington, November 29 – December 3, 1999, April 4, 2000.

Schnaubel, Christopher M. "Lessons in Command and Control from the Los Angeles Riots", *Parameters* (Summer 1997) 88-109

Townsend, Frances F., *The Federal Response to Hurricane Katrina: Lessons Learned*, February 23, 2006, Available from: http://georgewbush-whitehouse.archives.gov/reports/katrina-lessons-learned, Accessed February 17, 2011.

U.S. Constitution, Art. I, §8

U.S. Constitution, Art. II, §2

U.S. Constitution, Am II

U.S. Constitution, Am III

United States Northern Command, Missions, Available from: http://www.northcom.mil/About/history_education/vision.html. Accessed March 2, 2011.

Wolverton II, Joe., "Barack Obama Continues Bush Administration Policy Regarding Posse Comitatus," *The New America Magazine*, October 30, 2009,Available from: http://www.thenewamerican.com/index.php/usnews/politics/2195-barack-obama-continues-bush-administration-policy-regarding-posse-comitatus, Accessed: February 15, 2011.

Woodard, Timothy J., Lieutenant Colonel (Retired) 81st Separate Infantry Brigade S-2, Washington Army National Guard, telephone interview with author March 11, 2011.

10 United States Code §371-381

10 United States Code §375

10 United States Code §1385

18 United States Code §831

18 United States Code §382

www.ingramcontent.com/pod-product-compliance
Lightning Source LLC
Chambersburg PA
CBHW080808290526
45790CB00008B/3610